MIRRORS

OF
THE SUN

FINDING REFLECTIONS OF LIGHT IN THE SHITTINESS OF LIFE

CHLOE,
HERE ARE SOME BITE
SIZED POEMS PACKED
WITH RADIANCE !!
ENJOY !!
Curt

CURTIS TYRONE JONES

Copyright © 2017 by Curtis Tyrone Jones
All Rights Reserved.

This book is protected under the copyright laws of the United
States of America. Any reproduction or other unauthorized use of
the material or artwork herein is prohibited without the express
written permission of the author.

First Printing: July, 2017

Book Design by Maureen Cujatar
www.gopublished.com

Cover Design by Angie Alaya
www.fiverr.com/pro_ebookcovers

Crystal Style Sun Icon Vector
freedesignfile.com/51447-crystal-style-sun-icon-vector

Table of Contents

PART 2: MIRRORS OF THE SUN

Introduction

I recently had the opportunity to speak with a good friend; a doctor, who from time to time works with cancer patients whose faces, mouths, and necks have been eaten away by cancer. The potential for pain and deformity in these people's lives can be horrendous—physically, socially, and emotionally. It is not uncommon for such patients to be missing eyes and noses, likening the faces of these everyday people to Harvey Dent; the fictional character in Batman who was nicknamed Two-Face after acidic chemicals were maliciously thrown at the left side of his face. However, there is nothing fictional about the realities that these individuals must face, day in and day out, throughout the life of their illness.

Furthermore, the growths that can form in and around the mouth coupled with the location and depth of the facial scarring sustained over time can prevent proper hygiene and/or make wound care very complicated. All of this can leave odors that can be offensive even to the most seasoned medical staff. While speaking with the doctor who works with these individuals, I asked, "Does it ever bother you, Doc?" Without hesitation and with complete sincerity, she replied, "No. It doesn't bother me at all. Because when I go into the rooms of all my patients, I don't see *patients*, I see radiant souls. The people that I see who have portions of their faces destroyed by cancer remind me of the title of a book that I once read called 'Till We Have Faces'.[i] The faces that they now have are not their true faces, I see each person for who they really are."

I responded to the doctor by saying, "Your words remind me of similar concept by the same author. He wrote that if we were to see our neighbors in the fullness of who they are, we would be tempted to bow down and worship them because they would be so glorious."[ii] The doctor responded, "That's it! That's how I see my patients! They are radiant!" In one instance, after hearing her patient's story and addressing the patient's questions and medical concerns with compassion and care, the doctor voiced some closing words and parted with a kiss; a gesture she does from time to time, which communicates deep acceptance and solidarity with patients and their families. However, on this occasion, unbeknown to the doctor, the spouse of this patient, commented to another medical representative that, "She (the doctor) was an absolute angel to us both."

This story can be a blueprint for the relational mirroring process that I want to express in this book. These harsh life circumstances provide overwhelming opportunities for this man and his family to identify more with the shittiness of their situation than with finding opportunities to experience deep and meaningful connection in the midst of a devastating time. However, this family did not let the darkness of their hardships keep them from missing the light of this beautiful human encounter. The doctor sees her patients not as patients—defective, broken, or damaged individuals—but rather, sees them in their essence. She sees them as radiant individuals, in the highest form of their humanity, filled with dignity and worth. In return, those under her care also see her as being equally radiant because, as human as they may appear to us, angels are nothing if not dazzlingly radiant.

Though I have never met anyone who has been able to consistently view and treat all others in the highest capacity of each person's radiance at all times and in every aspect of life, this should not be a hindrance to the goal of this book. As the ancient Buddhist metaphor goes, "The master is a finger that points to the moon. If you focus on the finger, you can't see the moon."[iii] *Mirrors of The Sun* was written to be a reminder of our true nature and a challenge to live into that nature regardless of how bright or dim we understand ourselves to be in this present moment.

Relational mirroring sees the highest qualities of the other, names it, and calls it forth. However, there is another kind of mirroring that is just as important. This second kind of mirroring has been well portrayed in the stunning image of the tiny kitten who stumbles upon a puddle of spilled water in the house of its owner. What the kitten sees in its reflection in the puddle is a spitting image of itself in the form of a similarly-striped, full-grown tiger peering back at it.[iv] I will refer to this second kind of mirroring as *individual mirroring* because the focus is on each individual seeing the magic of self-discovery and summoning their greatest potential from the depths of themselves.

The caption that usually accompanies these memes, which have been duplicated in many settings with various humans[v] and animals[vi] alike, usually says something along the lines of, "What matters most is how you see yourself". If my previous literary work, *Giants At Play*, was written for you to see yourself as a giant and thereby learn to live into the largeness of your destiny, *Mirrors of The Sun* was written for you to see yourself as a massive entity of radiance that helps you to define yourself as a creature of your own unique enlightenment and encourages you to define everything else in existence by that light that you shed upon it in the dawning of your own particular self-love.

MIRRORS
OF SUN
THE

"I wish I could show you when you are lonely or in the darkness, the astonishing light of your own being." ~ Hafiz[vii]

"Our deepest fear is not that we are inadequate. Our deepest fear is that we are powerful beyond measure. It is our light, not our darkness that most frightens us. We ask ourselves, Who am I to be brilliant, gorgeous, talented, fabulous? Actually, who are you *not* to be? You are a child of *infinity*. Your playing small does not serve the world. There is nothing enlightened about shrinking so that other people won't feel insecure around you. We are all meant to shine, as children do. We were born to make manifest the glory of *the universe* that is within us. It's not just in some of us; it's in everyone. And as we let our own light shine, we unconsciously give other people permission to do the same. As we are liberated from our own fear, our presence automatically liberates others." ~ Marianne Williamson (adapted).[viii]

PART ONE
The Strength Of Self-Discovery

The Strength Of Self-Discovery

Somehow I won
in a game of tug of war
with the sun,
& discovered I'd been
underestimating the strength
of my own light
for entirely
too
long.

Flavoring The Future

Wise is the one
who flavors the future
with some salt
from the past.
Becoming dust is no threat
to the phoenix
born
from the ash.

Cultivating Comfort

Bright is
the one who is
comfortable
in the
darkness.

Whispering Diamond

You are a
whispering diamond,
turning in the sun, articulating
the one thing the sky
wants to say,
in a million different
ways.

Cosmic Stirrings

A mind so wide,
the Big Dipper sinks
its ladle inside, to stir
the heart of humanity
with just a pinch of
light from a few
thousand
galaxies.

Gushing With Light

How is it
you're so ensconced
with the darkness of earth,
when I sit here like your moon
gushing with the light
of your infinite
worth?

Puddle Jumping

Life's
a gloomy puddle,
until you start
jumping
in it.

Roots Of Confidence

Dig deep & pull
the roots of confidence
from the ground of your being,
standing firm in the raging storm
until sunlight blossoms
inside you.

Waxing Elegance

I'm jazzed
on your moonlight.
Please don't let the darkness
ever hush your waxing
elegance.

Journey Of A Sun Goddess

After dark
she came out of hiding
& set fire to her fears;
Vibrant, the sun
with her rays
of golden
hair.

Luminescent Life Force

There's a
luminescent life force
pulsating in your eyes,
enlightening me with
the possibility that
I too can survive—
Anything.

Shadowing The Moon

Live
in the shadow
of the moon,
until you're
bright enough
to give birth to
your own
suns.

Scattered Dreams

My radiant soul
summoned me to
awaken to the darkness
of my scattered dreams,
which were brighter &
more spacious
than my cluttered
reality.

Summer Solstice

The sun never sets
on you my summer solstice.
The longest day since you
arose upon my life
& I too will
never
come down.

Aftermath

You're such a
beautiful disaster,
the darkness flees
the aftermath of
your elegant
laughter.

The Never-Ending Night

You can't
stop dreaming
just because the
night never
seems to
end.

Passion's Matchbox

Passion
has infinite ways
to strike you against
its matchbox, but you
can't seem to take
your mind off of
yesterday's
dying
embers.

Symphonic Masterpiece

Sun rays
play passionately
upon her face, like
busy fingers trying to awaken
an experienced audience
to a symphonic
master-
piece.

New Mirrors

Most
of the time
we don't need
new images,
we just
need
new
mirrors.

Wings Of Enlightenment

You always
drop by, to enlighten
my mind, when my wings
are feeling heavy
& I've forgotten
how to
fly.

Odyssey Into Your Oddity

Your oddity is
your hottest commodity
but you scratch yourself
like it's the lottery
to reject yourself mentally,
spiritually,
&
bodily.

Imagination's Escalators

Take
imagination's
escalators
to the moon & rain dance
to the pulsating sun,
until you become
saturated
with the lightness
of an
astonishing
one.

Light Trip

Plummeting
into the farthest
parts of darkness
is always
a light trip
with
you.

The Enlightened Guillotine

The sun sacrifices
its pride to the
guillotine of the night,
realizing darker
perspectives can
often be
just
as bright.

Binging & Purging

You were out binge-
drinking bad self-esteem,
I slip my poetry in your cup
& watch you make love to
your self-image,
satisfying inner
pleas.

Suns Of Kindness

Dawn & burn with
such massive largeness
that your kindness
shines uncontainable
outside of both sides
of all small-minded
arguments.

Doors Of Depression

My heart
kept knocking
in search of you today.
The sun was
peeking in the window
for you to
come out & play.
But you were
avoiding us,
my
love.

Cracked

Sometimes
it's the cold &
broken shack that lets
the most love seep
through the
cracks.

Illuminate

Embrace
the empty space,
until the darkest
parts of your heart
are suddenly
illumined with
a galaxy
of
stars.

Travel Light

We travel light
despite the weighty
darkness of existence
that falls upon us
like night.

Tombs Of Light

So dead inside,
until your heart spoke
to you from its tomb of light,
& dawned on the lines in
your face, revealing
poetic
insight.

Ashing The Sun

Thoughts so high
on love they try to ash
the cherry of the sun
in the tray of the moon,
forgetting this is
the bush
never
consumed.

Gifted Mystic

Life's a gifted mystic.
Dare to resist its encryptions,
or tame the shooting star,
& ride further
into the depths
of who
you are!

Further

Love keeps
peeking through
the clouds
& pulling us
further
into
its
brightness.

Standing Against The Night

I'm still learning
the science of your
quiet defiance,
but I must say, "I'm
infatuated with the way
your soft luminosity
stands against
nightfall."

Riot

My mind is
a riot, torchlit with
every rowdy
thought of you,
blazing bright
inside
it.

Unraveling With Delight

A poet is someone
whose words can grasp,
& pull the thread of
a person's soul
& make them unravel
with delight.

Shadowboxing

Scrubbing vigorously,
he couldn't whitewash
his past. So he befriended it
like the old shadow
who walks with one
on new
paths.

Touching The Earth

My mind's
like earth
& keeps spinning
for you to touch
every part of it
with your
sunlight.

Hidden Immensity

Infinity peeks
into humanity & sees
itself immediately,
but we pick ourselves
apart ceaselessly
& never see the
hidden
immensity.

The Icing Of Silence

Squeeze the
icing of silence
all over the pastry of life,
so you grow light on word diets
in dark corners, satisfying
your gluttonous
appetite.

Cosmic Pilgrimage

It's funny
how you doubt yourself
through & through,
when the sun & the moon
are parabolically on a
pilgrimage,
encircling the mecca
of you.

Drenched In Wonder

As a poet,
all I can do
is pour ink buckets
of creativity
all over you,
until you're
drenched
in
wonder.

Storms Of Genius

Flashes of lightning
stretch across the
expanses of your mind
& strike you
with genius
of an
unknown
kind.

Bloom

Shower
each other
in brilliance
& watch the
way you
bloom.

Axis Of Spring

I love watching
the flower heads
in your heart
spring into bloom,
when you
tilt towards me
& my love
starts
warming you.

Flight Upon The Night

May the hand
of the moon be the guardian
that leads you to the chasm of your
darkest fear & teaches you
to soar upon
the night.

Cratered Fears

We only fear
peering down into the massive
canyons of life because
this fear of heights
exposes the mirrored
fear of depths
within.

Fertilizing The Darkness

I keep growing in
my darkness
because you keep
fertilizing it
with
the stars.

Caffeinated

Most nights,
you'll find me
swinging in the
hammock of the
moon, sipping
the night black,
a few stars
as sugar
cubes.

Radiant Teardrops

You brought
me your darkness
& I loved you
with the radiant
tears of a
thousand suns.

PART TWO
Mirrors Of The Sun

Mirrors Of The Sun

I keep
holding up
the mirror of the sun,
so you can see the stunning
reflections of everything
you're becom-
ing.

Radiant Wreckage

You see yourself
as a shipwreck, but we
see your treasure glowing inside,
beneath the oceans in
your eyes.

Explosions In The Night

I'm gonna
pack you into my
verses & set fire to the charge,
until you explode into the night,
recognizing the fireworks
you are.

The Story Of Generations

When she smiles,
the lines in her face
become epic narratives
that trace the stories
of generations
that no book
can
replace.

Chained To The Sun

Bound to the
mysterious radiance
of the whispering sun,
until this ball & chain
makes me a master
of my inner
one.

Diamonds Of Creativity

Each time
we bow to the feet
of anything
we find riveting,
the mind rises
to be surprised with
new crowning
diamonds
of
creativity.

Awakened Determination

Wake up!
Lay claim
to your dream with
sacred determination
flashing in your eyes,
never to play small
for the rest of
your life.

Somewhere

The stars
keep urging us
further into the darkness
with promises of finding
hidden brightness
somewhere deep
within
ourselves.

Suffering Eyes

I'm entranced
by your suffering eyes,
& your warmhearted smile
holds a dazzling capacity
for casually
mastering tragedy
inside.

Gifted Wings

And the night
loves to see you
on the edge & chasm of eternity,
pioneering flight
with the magnificent
wings of your
beautiful
gift.

Night Storming

Lost in your
night storm, leaping
from star to star,
madly interrogating
every tear to find
the place of emptiness
where you
are.

Mesmerizing

On your worst days,
the sun still gets
frustrated with wonder
at the simplicity of your
mesmerizing
radiance.

Burning Down The Night

And we have
every right
to keep burning
down the night,
until we find that
place of peace
in the captivity
of our
lives.

Barrels Of Light

So enamored
drinking the lantern
of intoxicating
grammar. Slurred speech
stuttered & stammered
as light leaked from
the barrels of
our
minds.

Kerosene Wick

My heart's
the kerosene wick
that's fortunate
to be torchlit by your
ravenous love,
flittering & dancing
all over
it.

Questioning The Night

When dusk falls
on my life, you sit there
so poised, still, & bright;
a second sun, setting a
question mark
against my
Dark. Weary. Night.

Shattered Reflections

Words like a mirror
shatter your calm exterior
& keep you beautifully
breaking
inside.

Dust

Unravel
my magic carpet.
Shake the gold-dust
from my trips to the sun
& take it for a spin
to the center
of your universe;
Within.

The Enlightened Finger

In a delightful mood,
bungee-jumping off the moon,
I'm a yoyo hurled from
the enlightened finger,
sloppy drunk on love's
intoxicating
danger.

Inferiority Complex

The sun
never has an
inferiority complex.
It shines the same
whether above
or
below.

Chancing Across The Sky

An incessant
aching for reawakening.
Creatively taking chances
to walk across the morning
& somehow brighten
up your
world.

The Dawn Of Freedom

Live so
radiant & free
that the sun longs
to come sit at your feet
to bask in the mentor-
ship of your soul's
experiential
gift.

Stethoscopic Sounds

My palms
warm the cool
stethoscope of the moon,
so I can listen to your heart
& write a poetic
prescription
for you.

Jazzed

We
belong to the sun,
who'll help us become
deaf to criticism
& jazzed
on
life.

Masks Of Brightness

She decorates
her face with the
mask of brightness,
that she wore
before the dawn
stole her innocent
laughter.

Light Up

We light up
around anyone
who makes us feel
screwed in,
to the
universe.

Everlasting Love Affair

The sun
still lives his silent
vows to the moon,
by bowing to kiss her feet
whenever she
walks
in
the room.

Combustible Clawings

Dance in the
darkness, until
your insides give their
trust to the combustible
things clawing their
way out of your
drowning
hardships.

Aligning Constellations

Time slowed down,
the universe aligned
& a constellation
of imagination dawned
upon the
creative mind.

Celestial Architectures

The architecture
of your thought
is so astonishing,
I want to walk
through
you.
Forever.

Centered

Let's just relax
into the magnificence
at the center
of our
being.

Myths Of The Sky Princess

After dark,
freckled with the stars,
the sky princess
tells stories through
ancient constellations
to help give
meaning
to
ours.

Blinding The Sun

A third eyelid
was torn inside.
A wide smile peaked out
& the sun went blind,
escorted across the starry asphalt
of the night sky
by a
big-hearted
child.

Charms & Enchantments

Poetic bliss
from the lips of a
charming prince
aroused her sleeping beauty
from the enchantments
of a poor self-
image.

Scribbled Anthems

Enticed by the night
setting upon our life,
gone astray, walking away
in search of anthems
scribbled by phantoms
of inner
rays.

Puzzled & Shattered

Puzzled,
I shattered, looking into
the mirror of the sun;
scattering my pieces to
the broken reflections
of whatever I
become.

Fire To The Night

When the moon's
lips touch my dreams
for a farewell kiss goodbye,
I become the yawning sun
that sets fire
to
the night.

Shades Of Sunflowers

The head of
all flower heads
is one flower;
the sunflower in the sky,
that gives the others
vivid color
stemming
from
the
inside.

Galaxies Of Family Trees

We've come
together
in love inseparable
to create
this stardust nebula
of which
there is no replica
in the
galaxies
of
family trees.

The Light Of Your Wingspan

There isn't
one sun in the
universe that's felt
more luminous than
the way my wings feel
perched under the
dawning of
your royal
plum-
age.

Hidden Faces

Nothing compares
to becoming aware of the
massive face of the universe
hidden in a newborn's
stare.

Useless Agitations

Hating yourself
is like hating the sun.
No matter how much
you complain of it
agitating your eyes,
its brilliance
shines
on.[ix]

Spun

Pole-vaulting
from cloud to cloud
we linger here on cloud-9
& plunge our straws
into the sun,
sipping radiance
until we're
spun.

Reverberating Whispers

The philosophy
in your eyes
is a catastrophic event
reverberating in my mind,
saying, "Take
a chance with fate,
before
it's too . . . ."

Burning Matches

Eclipsed by a dark
kingdom. Pen scratches
are my only matches
that burn with
love for me
like
the sun.

Chained To The Moon

Destiny
tied me to you,
my sweet lovely moon.
But the heaviness
of this ball & chain
enlightens my existence
while I'm submerged
here in utter
darkness.

Smashed Glass

Her heart is
smashed glass. Peer
into her jagged edges
to see what refracts
from the light of her past.
Kaleidoscopic
beauty.

Finding Sanity

You love
watching stars
rip out my heart
& present it to you
as a medallion of light—
when everything
in you is lost,
for
words.

Scattered Wholeness

The happy knuckles
of the moon plunge every
part of me in darkness,
until fragmented horizons
rise in the wholeness
of you.

Journeys In The Night

We journeyed
into the night
unprepared for life,
but the moon
held us in her vision,
until we reflected
her floating
wisdom.

Above Controversy

The sun was the
cherry of God's pipe,
which kept him
so high—
above
controversy.

Elephants In The Room

At midnight,
a herd of wild elephants sit
encircled around a campfire
whispering absurdities & dying of laughter
in the depths of my belly. When
they trumpet the raucous joy of their
existence, my heart is the
full moon that dances
in the
sky.

Purified Dreams

May the sun
purify your dreams
& continue
bringing out infinite things
from the depths
of your
bottomless
heart.

Heart Of Radiance

Our daughter
is the earth in space
between moon & sun.
We merge as one heart
between her lungs
& pump radiance
to whoever
she
becomes.

Painting The Sky

All my life
I've painted the sky
with the masterpiece
of my youthful leaves.

Now, my sun,

Rake me into
a cloud of infinities,
at my
comple-
tion.

Smoking The Sun

The moon
pours love in
my jar. The highest
one smokes the sun.
At dusk, we all see the
purple haze on
cloudy
horizons.

Clanging Against Nightfall

As one,
the moon & the sun
clang against the nightfall—
Bells tolling loud,
colored clouds,
silently
signal
the
day is done.

Crowning Sunsets

As it comes down,
carefully situate the sun
on yourself like a paper crown,
so the light of the universe
never sets
on
your dreams.

Special Acknowledgements

A massive thanks to the Twitter writing communities that helped to inspire the writing of so many poems in this book. Mirrors Of The Sun could not exist without the collective inspiration of Fieryverse, Madverse, Soulhoot, Heartsoup, Sensewords, Ashverse, and countless other sites and writers on Twitter who deeply influenced it.

Discover Previous Titles

Giants At Play: Finding Wisdom, Courage, & Acceptance To Encounter Your Destiny

Connect

INSTAGRAM
www.instagram.com/curtistyjones

TWITTER
twitter.com/CurtisTyJones

Notes

[i] C.S. Lewis, Till We Have Faces (Orlando: Harcourt, Inc.).

[ii] C.S. Lewis, The Weight Of Glory (New York: Harper One, 2001) 45.

[iii] Lao Tzu & Stephen Mitchell, Tao Te Ching: A New English Version (New York: Harper Audio, 2009).

[iv] "Believe in yourself", image accessed on May 20, 2017, https://goo.gl/KOmZcn.

[v] Image accessed on May 20, 2017, https://goo.gl/xZZSCk.

[vi] "What matters most is how you see yourself", image accessed on May 20, 2017, https://goo.gl/o26TET.

[vii] Daniel Ladinsky, I heard God Laughing: Poems of Hope and Joy/ Renderings of Hafiz. (New York: Penguin Books, 2006) Kindle file.

[viii] Marianne Williamson, A Return To Love: Reflections on the Principles of A Course in Miracles (New York: Harper Collins Publishers, 1992) 191.

[ix] Curtis Tyrone Jones, Giants At Play (self-published, 2014) 183.

77677540R00075

Made in the USA
Columbia, SC
03 October 2017